Chicago's Grand Hotel
A HISTORY OF THE HILTON CHICAGO

ISBN: 0-9723422-0-6 Hardcover Edition
0-9723422-1-4 Paperback Edition

Produced by Moonlight Publishing, LLC
Lafayette, Colorado

Book Design by Ann W. Douden
Boulder, Colorado

Printed in China

Chicago's Grand Hotel
A HISTORY OF THE HILTON CHICAGO

by

ROBERT V. ALLEGRINI

and

GERALDINE HEMPEL DAVIS

foreword by

RICHARD M. DALEY

Mayor of Chicago

RICHARD M. DALEY, MAYOR OF CHICAGO

For the past 75 years, the Hilton Chicago has been a Chicago landmark. Since the property opened as the Stevens in 1927, this venerable structure, which was then the largest hotel in the world, has reflected the spirit and vitality of our city. In its early years, the hotel played host to American icons like Babe Ruth, Amelia Earhart and Charles Lindbergh. It accommodated thousands of guests during the 1933 Century of Progress Exhibition and housed thousands of soldiers when the hotel was used by the military during the Second World War. When Conrad Hilton took over the hotel in the mid 1940s, it regained its pre-war glory and quickly became the site of some of Chicago's most important events.

The source of many fond memories for me and my family, the Hilton Chicago has been an important center of social and political life. In its current incarnation as the Hilton Chicago, the hotel maintains a vital role in our city. It serves as a major convention headquarters that supports Chicago's position as the convention capital of the nation. The hotel has also starred in numerous movies and television programs that have helped to spread the fame of Chicago worldwide.

I am pleased to present *Chicago's Grand Hotel: A History of the Hilton Chicago*, a chronicle of the fascinating history of this unique hotel and offer best wishes on your 75th anniversary celebration.

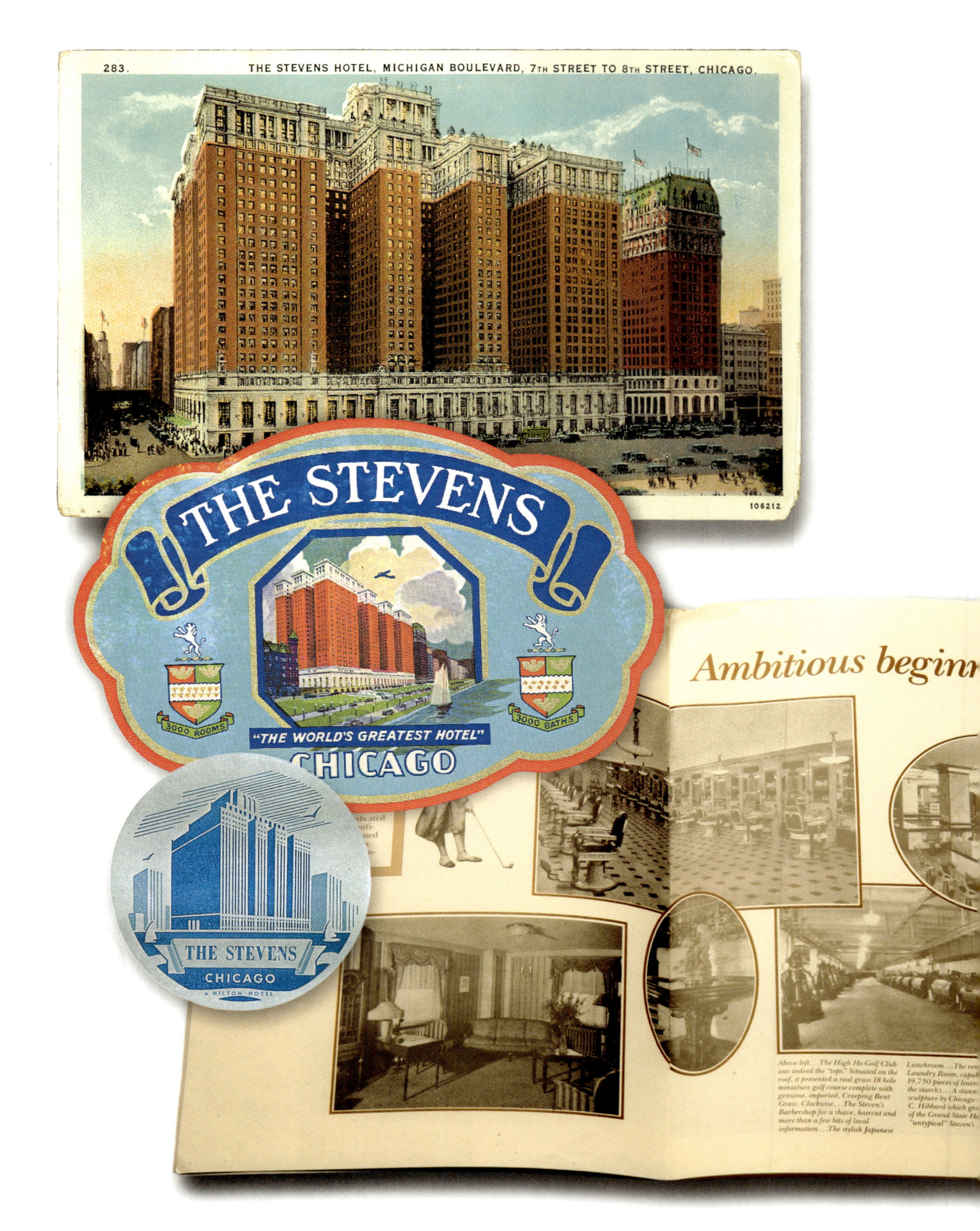

283. THE STEVENS HOTEL, MICHIGAN BOULEVARD, 7TH STREET TO 8TH STREET, CHICAGO.

106212

THE STEVENS

3000 ROOMS

3000 BATHS

"THE WORLD'S GREATEST HOTEL"

CHICAGO

THE STEVENS

CHICAGO

A HILTON HOTEL

Ambitious beginn

Above left...The High Ho Golf Club
was indeed the "tops." Situated on the
roof, it presented a real grass 18 hole
miniature golf course complete with
genuine, imported, Creeping Bent
Grass. Clockwise...The Steven's
Barbershop for a shave, haircut and
more than a few bits of local
information...The stylish Japanese

Lunchroom...The re
Laundry Room, capa
19,750 pieces of linen
the starch)...A stunn
sculpture by Chicago
C. Hibbard which gra
of the Grand Stair Ha
"untypical" Steven's

"THE WORLD'S GREATEST HOTEL"

"No one can predict what the changes of the next century will bring forth. It may be that today's wonder a hundred years from now will seem archaic, but the fact remains that this colossal structure ... this masterpiece of Bedford stone, steel girders, brick, cement, and marble, has been built to withstand the wear and tear of ages."

—*"A Trip Through The Stevens"*, Paul T. Gilbert, 1927

From the beginning, the Hilton Chicago was destined to be different. The vision of its founders and first namesakes, James W. Stevens and his son Ernest, The Stevens Hotel cost $30 million to build and opened its doors in May of 1927. Taking up an entire city block from Seventh to Eighth Streets on Michigan Avenue, the hotel fulfilled the Stevens's dream to create an entirely self-sufficient city within a city, and a place that would offer the world's most extensive convention facilities for the next fifty years.

Chicagoans first learned of the prospective hotel in *The Economist* of March 3, 1922. Under a bold headline that simply read "$15,000,000," the article told of the purchase of the Michigan Avenue property from the Otto Young Estate for $2,500,000, and the ambitious plan to build a hotel that would simply be "the largest in the world." The project was financed through the issuance of common and preferred stock in the name of The Stevens Hotel Company (whose president was James W. Stevens), and the Chicago architectural firm of Holabird and Roche was retained to "interpret Mr. E.J. Stevens's plans for a 'perfect' hotel."

The Stevens family presides at the grand opening of the hotel in 1927.

Breaking ground for The Stevens on August 25, 1925.

inset: The Stevens starts to take shape in April of 1926.
bottom: Grant Park and the Field Museum from the roof of the newly completed Stevens Hotel.

Speaking to workers at a flag raising ceremony at the building site in 1926, the younger Stevens said that "each of you have had an important part in erecting one of the most complicated and difficult structural steel jobs in the history of the building industry … Nearly twenty thousand tons of steel have been set, the first load of structural steel arriving on the job, Monday, November 9, 1925, just a few days less than six months ago." Out of gratitude for the hard work done so far, and as a reminder of the "part you played in the construction of the largest and finest hotel in the world," Stevens then handed each worker an envelope full of cash.

The completed Stevens Hotel had 3,000 "homelike" rooms and rose to twenty-eight stories. East facing rooms overlooked Grant Park and Lake Michigan. Five sub-basements contained the "engine room" of the hotel, where the laundry, the heating and cooling systems, and the carpentry, electrical, and plumbing shops could be found. The hotel also boasted a rooftop miniature eighteen-hole golf course, a hospital consisting of two wards

The Stevens Hotel was the Babe Ruth of the hotel world, racking up statistics that would remain unsurpassed. Among them:

✔ If you slept in every room of The Stevens Hotel for just one night, you would end up living there for more than eight years.

✔ An "amphibian plane ramp" directly in front The Stevens gave guests the option of arriving by air.

✔ It took 195 employees to maintain the laundry, washing and drying 328,000 pieces of linen daily.

✔ Seventy-two operators ran the twenty-five elevators, one of which was large enough to transport a ten ton truck.

✔ The Stevens required seventy-five telephone operators, more than would be required of a town of 25,000 in 1930.

✔ The initial order for The Stevens's china—manufactured by the Scammell China Company of Trenton, New Jersey—was for 300,000 pieces.

✔ Seven freight cars were required to ship the glassware from the Bryce Brothers plant in Pennsylvania.

✔ Ten two-story houses of five rooms each could be put in the Grand Ballroom.

✔ 50,000 yards of carpet, supplied by Hardwick & McGee, were used in the bedrooms alone. This did not include the beautiful oval bathroom carpets woven with The Stevens' crest.

Single and double guest rooms in 1927.

The High-Ho Golf Club—Located on the Roof of the Stevens—300 Feet Above Michigan Avenue

The Stevens
Michigan Ave., Sky

and an operating room, a 1,200-seat theater with "talking motion picture equipment," a five-lane bowling alley, a twenty-seven seat barbershop, and its own ice cream and candy factories. Perhaps the most stunning achievement of the builders was to create a Grand Ballroom that was completely free of visible structural pillars. An elaborate system of underground supporting pillars, caissons, and trusses supported the twenty-two stories of hotel above the ballroom. The trusses themselves each spanned eighty-six feet and weighed 240 tons.

The lobby of the hotel featured three different varieties of marble: gray Tennessee marble for the floor, red Levanta marble in the walls, and Botticino marble, imported from Italy, in the pillars. From the ceiling of the Grand Stair Hall, "painted in frescoe style suggestive of the late Renaissance," according to a Stevens brochure, hung chandeliers of bronze and crystal. The lounge combined "the best of the French periods in its architecture and furnishings" and contained three rare Saruk rugs. As Richard Cahan has written

above: "Fairyland," the playroom of The Stevens, in 1927. below: The Barber Shop at The Stevens. Nearby was the men's "manicure parlor" as well the office of the "chiropodist" in case of "foot trouble."

in his book, Chicago: Rising From the Prairie, "the hotel was large in scope, grand in design, and elegant in appearance."

To add further credence to The Stevens's reputation as a full service hotel, its many amenities made it quite possible for a guest to find all the necessities of life (and then some) within its walls. In addition to the golf course, theater, and barbershop, the hotel also contained a valet shop, a drug store that was open twenty-four hours a day, a house products shop (which after Prohibition ended served as the liquor store), a childrens' clothing and toy store, a beauty shop, a jewelry store, a haberdashery, a flower and candy shop, and a newsstand. Other facilities included a concert music library, a recreation room, a children's playroom ("Fairyland"), and a writing room. According to an early hotel brochure, many of these amenities were claimed to be "the largest and finest provided by any hotel in America today."

Its lending library, located on the fourth floor, contained thousands of volumes, and, according to the brochure, "Easy chairs, good light, a view of the

lake, a smoking room, an outside terrace for summer … [to] provide relaxation, entertainment and mental refreshment for the guest's free hours." A guest could check out a book and take it to their room, and so long as it was returned, would not be charged for it.

The checkroom for the Grand Ballroom alone could accommodate the coats and hats of 3,152 people. Three separate checking windows made it possible for large numbers of visitors to be accommodated "with alacrity and without confusion." Taking into account all of the public rooms, there was a total checking capacity of 6,000.

However, the largesse of the hotel was not limited to its massive structure and furnishings. According to *The Hotel World* (May 7, 1927):

> The guest, who registers at the desk and then goes immediately to his room, has had

Artists prepare murals for The Stevens in 1927.

nine employees working for him before the door of his room is closed and his establishment as a guest is concluded.

Each floor clerk on each of the twenty guest room floors is in charge of 136 rooms. These 136 rooms are divided into two units with 68 rooms in each unit. Each unit has 68 differ-

ent types of rooms and one half of the building is an exact duplicate of the other half, which gives the hotel two rooms alike in location, arrangement, decoration, size, and furnishings on each floor. From the first and lowest guest room floor to the twenty-fifth floor is exactly the same as the room in the same location twenty stories below it. Hence if a guest has a room on the tenth floor this week and likes it so well that when he returns two months later he asks for the same room which happens at the time to be occupied, it is possible to give him a selection of 39 other rooms which are exact duplicates of the one he last occupied.

Ernest Stevens himself designed the bathroom water faucets, featuring three spigots over each basin: hot and cold ones, naturally, but also a clever third faucet for ice water set above the ordinary ones. Also, each bathroom had a handy gadget permanently set in the wall tile that has become standard equipment in hotels and motels the world over: a

The dining room at The Stevens, later transformed into the Boulevard Room.

bottle opener. Evidently Mr. Stevens had seen enough furniture damaged from both failed and successful attempts to open bottles.

And all of this could be enjoyed at what today appear to be ludicrously low prices. A brochure dated November 15, 1928, offered room rates ranging from $3.50 to $10.00 a night for a single and from $5.00-$15.00 a night for a double. All with a private bath, of course. A modest breakfast in the Japanese Lunch Room would cost 45 cents, but if you wanted to splurge for dinner in the Main Dining Room, that would set you back all of $3.00. Adjusted for inflation, of course, these prices today would be much higher, but still competitive. The Stevens was, after all, a hotel for the people.

The Stevens officially opened its doors on the evening of May 2, 1927. Caught up in the moment, Ernest Stevens greeted visitors with words to match his creation:

> "Tonight, to the great city of Chicago we dedicate the realization of an ideal—the largest hotel on earth. We pledge to you that The Stevens will always provide rest,

refreshment and entertainment in such manner and in such measure that the stranger within our gates will feel that Chicago is not only great in material things but it is also host-friendly, hospitable, and kind."

The first guest to register was no less than the Vice President of the United States, Charles G. Dawes, followed by President Machado of Cuba. The Chicago Association of Commerce honored Machado with a luncheon on May 3rd for 2,000 in the Grand Ballroom; in his speech the Cuban President openly praised not only Cuban-American relations but the grandeur of The Stevens Hotel as well.

The first gala event at The Stevens took place on May 4, when the hotel hosted the Motion Picture Association Ball. In attendance were 3,000 movie stars and friends, among them Cecil B. de Mille and Victor McLagan, star of the film "What Price Glory." Thus began the hotel's long-standing reputation as a place comfortable for celebrities from all walks of life.

The Normandie Lounge as it appeared in the 1930s.

However, the most celebrated guest of that inaugural year was unquestionably Charles A. Lindbergh, who was honored by the City of Chicago at a dinner at The Stevens on August 13. Among the dessert offerings was "Glace Fantaisie a la Lindbergh," an icy concoction that no doubt played off of the Lone Eagle's heroic solo flight across the Atlantic earlier that year.

The Stevens was also host to less grand events that were still vital to the social life of Chicago. Here met the Chicago Wellesley Club, Alpha Iota Society and other fraternal groups; each evening countless small dinner dances took place in the various gathering rooms. Not a day or evening went by that there wasn't something going on at The Stevens.

In that first year, a young man by the name of Sam Cascio began working at The Stevens as a bellman. He was still there sixty-five years later, gaining the distinction of the "World's Oldest Working Bellman." (When asked about retiring, Cascio replied, "If I retire, I'm afraid I'll get old.")

Dinner in honor
of
Colonel Charles A. Lindbergh
by
The Mayor's Committee
of Chicago
and
The Chicago Association of Commerce
Saturday evening
the thirteenth of August
One thousand nine hundred and twenty-seven
The Stevens

ENU

DEW MELON
AND RASPBERRIES SUPREME
JELLO
—
ILLON, BELLEVUE
—
N BRANCHE
ISHES
CALIFORNIA MIXED OLIVES
SALTED ALMONDS AND PECANS
FILET OF LAKE SUPERIOR JUMBO WHITEFISH
EN ASPIC, BELVEDERE
BROILED SUPREME GUINEA-CHICKEN, CUMBERLAND
POTAT ASPARAGUS TIPS, D'ARGENTEUIL
STUFFED EN SURPRISE
MOUSSELINE
IE A LA LINDBERGH
MIGNARDISES
TASSE

above: Menu cover from a dinner given in honor of Charles A. Lindbergh just after The Stevens opened in 1927. right: Menu cover from a dinner given in honor of the Crown Prince of Denmark and Iceland in 1939.

The Danish National Committee
and
The Icelandic Association
of Chicago

Banquet
in honour of
Their Royal Highnesses
The Crown Prince and Crown Princess
of Denmark and Iceland
at the Stevens Hotel, Chicago
Tuesday, the twenty-fifth of April
One thousand nine hundred and thirty-nine

The Christmas 1931 issue of "Stopping at The Stevens," was the hotel's newsletter featuring items about recent guests, upcoming events, poetry, and book excerpts provided by the librarian.

STOPPING AT THE STEVENS

A Right Merry Christmas from The Stevens

DECEMBER 24, 1931

Vol. 10   No. 223

PUBLISHED BY THE STEVENS HOTEL COMPANY, CHICAGO, ILLINOIS

"Stopping at The Stevens," a chatty newsletter that appeared every couple of weeks, profiled important guests—such as James D. Bobbroff, representative of the Eversharp Lawn Mower Company—told of forthcoming events, and even included book excerpts from new arrivals in the library. Perhaps portentous of the difficult times ahead, the "Stopping at The Stevens" dated December 24, 1931, led off with this Christmas greeting:

"Out of the turbulence and unrest which have beset the world these many months there have been born a humble spirit, a sympathetic understanding of the problems of the poor, an appreciation of the cultural activities and a kinship with the spiritual. That all of the guests within our walls may share in the peace and comfort derived from these manifold blessings is our earnest hope on this joyous Natal day of Love."

Poetry was supplied by the newsletter's editor, Mrs. Grace Garraghan, who also encouraged guests "to visit the Editorial Offices on the 4th Floor to register their names for publication." Judging from the heft of several issues of "Stopping at The Stevens," many did just that.

. . . .

OVERHEARD . . .

in the check room the morning after the Motion Picture Association Ball:

"Oh! Mabel! You should have been here last night at the movie ball. The way the girls and women mobbed Milton Sills was a disgrace! How can they do it? Even Mr. Bluecoat, the tall man at the entrance, thought they were staging the mob scene from 'Men of Steel' as part of the ball, and he ran for his life. You know Mabel, Victor McLagan and George O'Brien came in, too, but nobody saw them. It was a fright the way those girls acted. But there is something so 'virile' about Milton Sills. I don't know what that means, but it is what *Photoplay* called him last week. He never flinched a bit. He just smiled, and when they got too rough he used the strong arm on them. Then he sent down to the checkroom for 3,000 checks—gave them to the girls and started calling their numbers for their dance with him. It was awful the way they acted, Mabel! My, but he is virile. I was wishing I didn't have on this new red dress so that I could get near enough just to feel his muscle."

If The Stevens rode the crest of the prosperous Roaring 20s, however, it was equally susceptible to the fallout from the Great Crash of 1929. Not soon after, as America entered the Great Depression, vacancies began increasing precipitously, and the Grand Ballroom and dining rooms stood silent and empty. Indeed, it is estimated that some eighty-one percent of the hotels in the United States went bankrupt during the Great Depression. The 1933 Century

Great Hall decorated for the opening of the Normandie Lounge.

of Progress Exposition (which actually lasted until October of 1934) gave the hotel a bit of a boost, but in June of 1934 The Stevens was declared insolvent, and the equity of the preferred and common shareholders was wiped out. Only the conversion of some of the rooms into apartments in 1935 as part of a reorganization plan kept the hotel afloat; by 1937 four floors had been converted. Still, the Depression had taken its toll. Built for $30 million, the hotel now appraised for only $7 million.

Hard times stayed with The Stevens until World War II, when the hotel, like the rest of the country, was pulled out of a decade-long slump by America's need to mobilize quickly to address the needs of the war effort. In fact, two events directly related to the war, and both occurring in 1942, had a lasting effect on the hotel.

The first took place in an unlikely setting: New York Harbor, where the Normandie, pride of the French line, caught fire as it was being converted from luxurious ocean liner to troopship during the winter of 1942. The fire began when an errant spark from an acetylene torch landed on a pile of highly flammable kapok life jackets on the afternoon of February 9. By about 2:45 A.M. on February 10, the Normandie had slid on to her port side and rested there at a seventy-nine degree angle. A year and a half later, the ship was at last righted, but many of her fixtures and furniture had been sold off. Among the buyers was The Stevens, which created "The Normandie Lounge" from the various items, and even built a mock bow of the ship as its entrance when the lounge debuted. The second event of 1942 was the purchase of The Stevens, for $6 million, by the U.S. Army for use as

With this notice the Army took over The Stevens in 1942.

classrooms and bar-racks for the Army Air Force Technical Train-ing School. The tak-ing over of hotels, a common occurrence during the war, not only helped hotel owners and the mili-tary, but it also aided the taxpayer, who

Because some classes slept while others worked, the soldier-residents of The Stevens were called to formation by a whistle instead of a bugle.

would be paying far more for the construction of a comparable new building. Indeed, Secretary of War Stimson estimated that the purchase of The Stevens saved the Army $475,000 a year. The sale was announced on December 13, 1942, and approved by a two-thirds vote of The Stevens Hotel Corporation shareholders shortly thereafter.

"Unit 1," as The Stevens was called in the military vernacular, had already been converted for use by the Army the preceding July. Guests were given two weeks "to seek housing elsewhere" and asked to

vacate by August 1. The hotel was emptied of any-one and anything connected to the hotel world; rooms became offices, classrooms, and barracks. The Oak Room became a civilian employment office. Brocades and other elaborate window treat-ments were taken down. The on-site drug store was made into a PX. The chandeliers were removed from the Grand Ballroom, and its floor was covered with linoleum; this became the mess hall. As one con-temporary magazine described the transformation, "The halls of the one-time Stevens Hotel now echo

MESS B-19

The great ballroom, of what used to be the Stevens Hotel — where many of the most brilliant functions of the middle west were held during the past 15 years — is now the B-19 Mess of the Chicago Schools, Unit No. 1. Operating 24 hours a day to feed the succession of classes, more than one-half of the students of the Chicago Schools mess in this enormous area once dedicated to conventions, meetings, balls and banquets. The room is 100 by 200 feet, seats over 2000 men at mess. Many chefs, including a number who served the hotel before the war, now devote their talents, under the supervision of Army Mess Officers, to seeing that the soldier students are fed promptly and well. Men are not limited to one helping. The only rule is "no waste".

...ny of the spacious areas ...both Unit No. 1 and No. ...ow post "dayrooms" for ...tion of soldier students. ...whenever a pianist sits ...

A balanced diet is ... of Chicago School, ... the Army. Chicago ... all they want to eat ... starches, carbohydra... is taken to have the ... pared. Hard work, b... the men big appetite... a day, serving brea... at three different ho...

The Stevens housed the men and women of the Army Air Forces Training Command for twelve months during World War II.

to the sharp whistle blasts of top sergeants and class leaders calling their men to formations." The hotel that once comfortably hosted 3,000 guests became home to 10,000 air cadets crowded three or four to a room. The hotel's Chief Engineer, Harold M. Toombs, recalled that he'd show an arriving officer to his room, "and four days later, I'd run across him wandering through the corridors, hunting for the place where he belonged. Lost as completely as he would be in a jungle, and no one to lead him out."

As suddenly as the Army took over The Stevens, it withdrew less than a year later, after graduating thirty classes of mechanics, meteorologists and instrument technicians. A patriotic advertisement taken out in *Chicago Skylines* on July 15, 1943, by area businesses (for whom the Army was no doubt a significant customer), announced, "The Stevens and Congress hotels are honorably discharged from military service and return to civilian use. It would be only fitting and proper, we think, that as a reminder to future guests, these institutions be permitted a service bar on their stationery in recognition of the part they played in the nation's emergency."

Just what would become of The Stevens at this point was the subject of much debate. Some suggested a federal building; others wanted to use it as rent-free housing for service wives with low incomes. Still others wanted to see it converted into a hospital—or a technical school. Finally, someone came along with an idea too obvious to appear credible: why not convert it back into a hotel?

The 1949 Clinical Congress meets in the Grand Ballroom.

75ᵗʰ ANNIVERSARY
BANQUET
POLISH ROMAN CATHOLIC UNION
September 20, 1948
Stevens Hotel ○ Chicago, Ill.

Members of the 1949 Clinical Congress watch television for the first time in the Normandie Lounge.

"REFITTING" THE STEVENS

Getting The Stevens up and running again after a year of military duty required scouring the country for 3,850 box springs and mattresses, 150,000 pieces of silverware, 300,000 pieces of china, 3,000 gold chairs, and four train car loads of glassware. The bedsprings proved particularly difficult to secure because the government hoarded steel for the war effort. However, the needs of The Stevens managed to move up the priority list, and 125,000 pounds of steel were ultimately released to make bedsprings.

A Stevens bill from 1947, showing what $46.35 could get you back then.

THE STEVENS
Chicago
A HILTON HOTEL

Nº K10391

Memo	Date	Explanation	Amt. Charged	Amt. Credited	Balance Due
			6.50		8.85
1	MAY 27-47	ROOM	6.50		8.85
2	MAY 27-47	RESTR	2.35		15.35
3	MAY 28-47	ROOM	6.50		25.09
4	MAY 29-47	RESTR	9.74		31.83
5	MAY 29-47	ROOM	6.50		33.11
6	MAY 29-47	PHONE	0.24		39.61
7	MAY 30-47	VALET	1.28		
8	MAY 30-47	ROOM	6.50		46.35
9	MAY 31-47	ROOM	6.50		0.00
10	MAY 31-47	PHONE	0.24	46.35	
11	JUN-1-47	PAID			
12					
13					
14					
15					
16					
17					
18					
19					
20					
21					
22					
23					
24					

We have tried to make your stay at THE STEVENS a pleasant and enjoyable one, and we hope the next time you come to Chicago you will let us know ahead of time so we can have just the type of accommodations you want ready for you. A warm welcome will be awaiting you.

Last balance is amount due unless otherwise indicated. Bills are payable when presented.

PAYMENT RECEIVED THANK YOU 1947 JUN 1 AM 9 00

That individual was Stephen Healy, a contractor and President of the Avenue Hotel Corporation. He purchased the building from the Army for $5,250,000 and promised to reopen the hotel by the end of 1943. By this time, of course, many of the hotel's original furnishings had been sold or auctioned, so the task of re-conversion was monumental. However, Healy was accustomed to big challenges. As the *Saturday Evening Post* noted in a feature article on the reborn hotel:

> Healy is a contractor—a big contractor. With Henry Kaiser and other associates, he had just dug the excavations for new locks at Panama … . He had blasted thirteen miles of Delaware aqueduct through solid rock. He had started a hydroelectric dam in Kentucky … . He was looking for an investment, and the big hotel, at twenty cents on the dollar of its original cost, seemed like a bargain.

The construction crew—Healy's own—would continually find valuable items stored in the basements, hallways, nooks, and crannies. 15,000 coat hangers

were discovered piled shoulder high in one of the bedrooms. Enough new carpet to cover two entire corridors turned up in its original wrappings. Due to the shortage of scrap metal, the locksmith despaired of having no material to make new keys—until he came across a full ton of keys that the Army had neatly stacked away. Three days before opening, it was discovered that 900 rooms had been booked but only 800 beds were available. Led by Head Carpenter Oscar Zigman, a crew built the necessary 100 beds out of scrap lumber.

Piece-by-piece The Stevens was put back together and soon restored to its former glory. Still, with many men and women lost to the war effort, Healy once again had to call upon his own people to simply make The Stevens operational. Richard J. Hill, an insurance man "whose view of hotel living had always been from the front side," was named manager. "I used to wake up at night and look out the window in the Blackstone across the street," he told the *Saturday Evening Post*, "and say to myself how can we ever get the damned thing going?" Marvin Orland, one of Healy's men in Panama whose specialty was handling dynamite, became the personnel director. Martin Davis, Healy's purchasing agent for such items as tractors, bulldozers, and turret lathes, was now in charge of ordering linens, silver, glass and china.

Of all the jobs that had to be filled at the rejuvenated hotel, that of chambermaid proved most difficult. One Sunday in early 1944 only eleven maids showed up to make beds for 2,700 guests. "When night came and four new lines of people stretched across the lobby," reported the *Saturday Evening Post,* "a sign was set up saying 'We are Having Maid Trouble. Please Make Your Own Bed.' Out of a big floor truck guests took sheets, pillow slips and towels, and not a one complained." The Healy men came through as well. One big Healy "tunnel man" by the name of Tim Cleary, struggling with the intricacies of tucked-in sheets, was asked "How are you coming, Tim?" by his sympathetic boss. "Don't call me Tim," he replied. Just call me Evelyn. That's me name on this job." Thus Healy's ex-construction men henceforth dubbed themselves "Evelyns."

The "Evelyns" were still around when The Stevens hosted both the Republican and Democratic national conventions in the summer of 1944. ("It's the first time the two parties ever agreed on anything," manager Dick Hill was to have said.) Though the con-

President's Day menu from the 1930s.

ventions were held a month apart, both parties maintained headquarters for several months at The Stevens, fourteen floors away from each other. "Neutral" ground was a floor where batteries of telephones and teletypes were readied for the 800 correspondents sent to cover both conventions. Only The Stevens, in 1944 still the world's largest hotel, could "cater to the whims of both Yankee Republicans and Southern Democrats."

A SUPREME MEMORY

Current U.S. Supreme Court Justice John Paul Stevens was just a boy of seven when his father, Ernest Stevens, and grandfather, James W., opened their spectacular new hotel. His memories include meeting both Charles Lindbergh and Amelia Earhart, as well his father's battles with the Ringling Brother's circus, which was set up across the street from the hotel in Grant Park. (The hotel eventually filed a complaint and the circus was moved to the south, thus restoring the vista between the hotel and Lake Michigan.) The hotel changed hands when Justice Stevens was about 12 or 13, but his daughter was married there shortly after the renovations of 1984–85.

The STEVENS

CHICAGO

WORLD'S LARGEST and friendliest HOTEL

THE STEVENS
BECOMES A HILTON

Eight years before The Stevens Hotel rose from the shores of Lake Michigan, a thirty-two year-old World War I veteran stumbled into the oil boomtown of Cisco, Texas and attempted to secure a room at the Mobley Hotel. Informed that the hotel didn't even have a sitting room, much less a room to sleep in, Conrad Nicholson Hilton decided to lean against a pillar in the lobby until a vacancy occurred.

(So popular was the Mobley during the Texas oil boom that the rooms turned over every eight hours.) When "a granite-faced gentleman" approached Hilton to warn him against loitering in the hotel, Hilton asked him if he owned the place. The rest of the story is recounted in Hilton's memoir, *Be My Guest*:

Crowds outside the Conrad Hilton greet General Douglas MacArthur in 1951.

The Great Hall of the Conrad Hilton prepared for General MacArthur to speak.

"I do," he said bitterly, [but] "I ought to be out there in the oil field making real cash."

"Are you saying," I spoke slowly … that this hotel is for sale?"

"Fifty thousand cash and a man could have the whole shooting match including my bed for the night."

"Mister, you've found yourself a buyer," I said.

Thus began one of the most remarkable achievements in the annals of American business. Following the purchase of the Mobley in 1919, his first hotel, Hilton went on to develop properties throughout Texas, culminating in the first hotel to bear his name, the Dallas Hilton, in 1925. He married shortly thereafter, and took his new bride on a transcontinental wedding trip that included Chicago. While there, he recalled in *Be My Guest*,

… Chicago had charms. "Some day," I told Mary, I'm going to come back and find a vacant lot. I'd like to build me a hotel here." I didn't know that someone, right that minute, was saving me the trouble; had found the vacant lot and was putting up The Stevens, the largest hotel in the world. It would be twenty years before I embarked upon the adventure of buying The Stevens. And it was quite an adventure.

That twenty-year interval saw Hilton make a small fortune, lose it, then regain it as America pulled

The Great Hall decorated for a flower show in 1945.

out of the Depression. In 1938 he bought the Sir Francis Drake Hotel in San Francisco. By 1943 he owned both the Roosevelt and the Plaza in New York. In the late 1930s his sights were once again set on Chicago: "I wanted the largest hotel in the world," he stated simply. So he purchased mortgage bonds on The Stevens at between 20 and 60 cents on the dollar as a way of eventually leveraging ownership. However, the takeover by the Army in 1942 put a bittersweet end to that; while he was no longer able to "get his foot in the door" to acquire The Stevens, the U.S. government paid him 100 cents on the dollar, plus interest, for the bonds. "That check for $400,000 was the largest I ever had in my life," he wrote.

After The Stevens reverted to private ownership in 1943, and had been transformed from a gigantic Army barracks back into a hotel by the enterprising Stephen Healy, Hilton announced to his mother one night that he had decided to go to Chicago on the next train, "and I'm going to stay there until I get The Stevens."

However, it was not to be so simple as that. Calling it the most "nerve-wracking, frustrating, ulcer-making" negotiation of his career, Hilton laid the blame at the feet of the "positively unpredictable business procedures of Mr. Stephen Healy." According to the way Hilton tells it in *Be My Guest,* he and Healy had shaken hands on a deal three separate times. "And

three times," Hilton wrote, "the two fisted dynamic contractor turned pixie and vanished into thin air, each time raising the ante." At first Hilton and Healy had shaken hands on a deal in which Healy would realize a $500,000 profit; Healy then thought it over and demanded a profit of $650,000. The two shook hands on the second deal. "Again Healy vanished only to reappear with more expensive ideas." Hilton and Healy shook hands for a third time when the stipulated profit rose to $1,000,000. When it came time to close the deal, Healy was not to be found.

Out of frustration, Hilton approached the owners of the Palmer House, determined to come away from Chicago with a hotel after all. It was during those negotiations that the suggestion was made that he acquire both hotels, but inasmuch as the Palmer management refused to have a "possible competitor" review its books, he was momentarily stymied. He deftly skirted this problem by declaring that it was his "firm conviction that Mr. Healy had no intention of selling" him The Stevens. Satisfied, the Palmer trustees agreed to proceed with negotiations following a due diligence of Hilton's "business methods, reputation, and past management records."

Diagram of the Hilton from the 1950s, showing the Tower Ballroom, now the Conrad Hilton Suite.

Home of the Famous BOULEVARD ROOM

THE **CONRAD HILTON**
CHICAGO

A luggage sticker touting the Boulevard Room and the Ice Show.

above:. Conrad Hilton the man unveils Conrad Hilton the hotel in a name changing ceremony.
below: Conrad Hilton greets a guest at his namesake hotel.

Turning his attention back to The Stevens, he complained to his colleague, Willard Keith, that he wanted both hotels, but feared he'd get neither. Keith simply cursed Chicago's snow and cold and suggested they return to California and think about it over a game of golf. "I don't go home until I get a hotel," Hilton declared. Keith thereupon trudged off "in the dismal remains of Chicago's last snowfall," only to return ninety minutes later with good news. He had found Healy and advised him that Hilton was buying the Palmer House instead of The Stevens. Healy thereupon settled upon a firm deal where he would sell the hotel for $7.5 million for a net profit of $1.5 million. The deal was closed shortly thereafter, even though Hilton discovered that The Stevens had only 2,673 rooms instead of the advertised 3,000, and also that Healy insisted on taking with him seventy-five cases of scotch and bourbon.

Hilton bought the Palmer House a few days later for $19,385,000, giving him both of Chicago's "crown jewels." Almost unintentionally, he had played one acquisition off the other, using the enigmatic Healy as his pawn.

Ice skaters perform in the Boulevard Room supper club in the 1950s.

The purchase of The Stevens by Hilton immediately elevated the hotel's reputation as a world-class facility capable of hosting conventions on a grand scale. It took its place alongside the Plaza, Roosevelt, Mayflower, and Palmer House as one of the signature hotels in the rapidly growing Hilton chain.

Hilton was committed to its development, sometimes in spectacular fashion: in the late 1940s he was persuaded by Hilton booking agent Merriel Abbott to build the largest ice stage ever in a hotel (though it still measured only 17 X 50 feet), and install a $125,000 sheet of mirrored glass in what was to become The Boulevard Room. Abbott, who was also responsible for booking acts into the Empire Room at the Palmer House, was looking for something "different" and had remembered that the original construction of the hotel included the capability for a built-in ice rink.

The Boulevard Room ice shows began a twenty-one-year run in 1948, featuring forty-three original "mini-musicals on skates." The music and lyrics to nearly all the productions were the product of a single composer, Hessie Smith, who unabashedly claimed that the shows were "the best family entertainment in the city."

It's not every hotel that can boast an ice show every day, but the Conrad Hilton did for many years in the Boulevard Room.

Guests stand for the arrival of Queen Elizabeth II in the Grand Ballroom.

Probably the greatest attribute Conrad Hilton brought to The Stevens was his own celebrity. Recalling its early years, The Stevens was once again host to film stars, politicians, and royalty, often personally welcomed to the hotel by Conrad Hilton.

Queen Elizabeth II arrives at the Hilton escorted by Chicago Mayor Richard J. Daley (left) and Conrad Hilton (right) in 1959.

The former husband of Zsa Zsa Gabor, and father-in-law to Elizabeth Taylor (for all of seven months in 1950), Hilton could call upon the stars of stage, screen, and the popular music scene to entertain at his hotels. Among the names casually dropped in *Be My*

President John F. Kennedy exits the Conrad Hilton Hotel with Chicago Mayor Richard J. Daley in the 1960s.

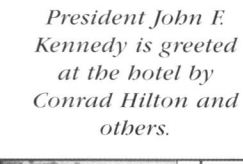

President John F. Kennedy is greeted at the hotel by Conrad Hilton and others.

Conrad Hilton with Republican Presidential nominee Barry Goldwater in 1964.

Vice President Richard M. Nixon speaks at the Conrad Hilton during the 1960 Republican National Convention.

Mayor Richard J. Daley toasts King Carl Gustav of Sweden at a Conrad Hilton banquet in the 1970s.
LASZLO L. KONDOR PHOTO

On January 14, 1969 the Chicago City Council honored the crew of Apollo 8 at the Conrad Hilton.

An astronaut festoons a cake in honor of Apollo 8.

Guest are Marge and Gower Champion, Eddie Duchin, Guy Lombardo, Benny Goodman, Tommy Dorsey, Jinx Falkenberg, and Mary Martin, all of whom had at one time or another performed at a Hilton hotel. The Stevens itself enjoyed such performers as Ella Fitzgerald, Dean Martin, and Nat King Cole entertaining at private parties.

Chicago celebrated "Apollo 8 Day" in 1969 with a luncheon in the Grand Ballroom of the Conrad Hilton.

CHICAGO CITY COUNCIL MEETING

Honoring

ASTRONAUT COLONEL FRANK BORMAN, USAF

ASTRONAUT CAPTAIN JAMES A. LOVELL, JR., USN

ASTRONAUT LT. COLONEL WILLIAM A. ANDERS, USAF

THE APOLLO 8 CREW

Tuesday, January 14, 1969

Brochure describing the 1962 renovations.

INTERIOR VIEW

A. International Ballroom
B. International Ballroom Foyer
C. Hotel Grand Ballroom
D. Continental Room
E. Continental Lobby — 8th Street
F. Exhibition Floor
G. Hotel Exhibition Hall

This is
HILTON CENTER
The Conrad Hilton Hotel's Magnificent New Addition
75,000 SQUARE FEET of NEW, SUPERB SPACE for
Conventions • Meetings • Conferences • Exhibitions • Banquets

EXTERIOR VIEW

Adjacent to and connected with The Conrad Hilton Hotel, on the northeast corner of Wabash Avenue and 8th Street in downtown Chicago, the building's exterior features white precast architectural panels, is of steel structure frame with concrete floor slabs throughout entire area.

Switchboard operators in the 1960s.

On July 27, 1960, guests were treated to a "Great Lady Luncheon Tableau" fashion show in the Grand Ballroom during the Republican National Convention.

All of this had a collateral effect on the growing reputation of The Stevens. Even so, Conrad Hilton insisted that he had "worked hard to buy The Stevens … worked even harder to give her a personality, a position in the life of her city, to change her from simply the largest hotel to the largest and friendliest." On November 19, 1951, as a "tribute to the inspiration, vision, and leadership of Conrad Hilton, President of the Hilton Hotels Corporation" the Board of Directors voted to change the name of The Stevens to The Conrad Hilton.

The new name was a charm. Among the first distinguished guests after the debut of the Conrad Hilton was General Douglas MacArthur, who gave a speech in the Great Hall following his return from Korea in 1951. That decade also saw visits from the likes of Bette Davis, Lauren Bacall, President

A menu from the dinner honoring Prince Phillip in 1966.

Eisenhower, and Senator John F. Kennedy. While guests at the hotel, people of prominence were frequently greeted by Richard J. Daley, Chicago's mayor from 1955-1976. However, the most distinguished guest of that era was undoubtedly Queen Elizabeth II, who made an official visit to Chicago in 1959. Photographs from the gala given in her honor in the Grand Ballroom show her accompanied by both Mayor Daley and Conrad Hilton.

The Conrad Hilton even made the *Guinness Book of World Records* during this period, earning its place in recorded history for serving the largest number of people at one meal: 7,200. This required all of the hotel's ballrooms and meeting space, as well 480 waiters. "The size of the tip," a brochure from the 1980s read, "was not disclosed."

Prince Phillip of the United Kingdom arrives at the Conrad Hilton for a dinner in his honor in 1966.

SEE THE ICE SHOW
THE BOULEVARD ROOM
THE CONRAD HILTON

IN THE
INCLUDING

Two-Day All-Expense

STUDENT EDUCATIONAL TOURS

OF CHICAGO for only $7.15

(PLUS 17c TRANSPORTATION TAX)

THE STEVENS HOTEL

The Conrad Hilton CHICAGO

Only $7.15* for two thrilling days in Chicago
ALL-EXPENSE STUDENT EDUCATIONAL TOURS INCLUDE

- Meals
- Room
- Sightseeing
- Tour Appointment
- Guide Service

FIRST DAY

SECOND DAY

For groups of 25 or more—plus 17c transportation tax.

Hilton 50th Anniversary 1927-1977

The advent of the 1960s saw further structural improvements. The number of rooms was reduced to 2,400 in 1960 in order to offer larger, more elaborate sleeping facilities, and in 1962 The Conrad Hilton completed construction of a $2.5 million convention complex. The three-level structure contained the International Ballroom, the world's largest, as well as 53,000 square feet of exhibit and/or meeting space. Combined with the convention facilities of the original hotel, the expanded Conrad Hilton now offered the largest convention and exhibit facilities of any hotel on earth. The meeting facilities could hold 15,000 people under one roof at one time, and the International Ballroom alone could hold 4,000 people for meetings, 2,600 for banquets, 2,200 for fashion shows, and 4,000 for dances.

The lobby of the hotel was completely restyled in 1968, and in 1970 its twenty-four manually operated elevators were converted to automatic, computer-controlled units for faster service.

Ever the hub of Chicago's social life, The Conrad Hilton became an unwit-

ting player in the political life of the city—and the nation—in the 1960s. A favorite among gathering Republicans and Democrats alike (eleven Democratic and fourteen Republican national conventions have been held in the city since 1860), the Hilton hosted the relatively sedate Republicans that nominated Richard Nixon in 1960, then became the eye of the storm as the Democrats gathered in August, 1968, where the "whole world watched" a city become unglued.

ROOM RATES IN 1955	
SINGLE with bath	$6.00 to $14.00
DOUBLE with bath	$10.00 to $18.00
TWIN with bath	$11.50 to $19.00
PARLOR BEDROOM and bath	$24.00 up
EXTRA BED IN ROOM	$4.00
DORMITORY style rooms available	
NO PETS ADMITTED	
PARKING FACILITIES Overnight $2.00	

The famous riots that turned Grant Park into a battlefield, and the Hilton into a triage unit, ironically had their origin in an event at the Hilton earlier that year, when before 2,200 people in the Hilton Ballroom President Lyndon Johnson announced that he would not be seeking re-election. Johnson's announcement opened the door for Vice President Hubert Humphrey to run, and though a prohibitive favorite, his support of the war in Vietnam split the party. Anti-war protesters gathered in Chicago to support their candidates, Senators George McGovern and Eugene McCarthy, but after failing to get permits to camp in Lincoln and Grant Parks, they clashed with police for five days over the right to use the parks.

The worst day of protesting was Wednesday, August 28, and came to be known as the "Battle of Michigan Avenue." Having been thwarted in their effort to march to the convention site, protesters confronted police on Michigan Avenue at Grant Park—virtually at the front doors of the Hilton, where the Democratic Party was headquartered and where many of the delegates were staying. The Chicago police had also set up a command post on the lower level of the hotel the day before the convention began. As both tear gas used by the police and "stink bombs" thrown by the protesters wafted into the lobby of the hotel, the decision was made to limit access and lock all the doors around the perimeter of the hotel. However, as then General Manager Bill Smith recalled, "this was a day long feat,

Vice President Lyndon Johnson arrives at the Conrad Hilton in early 1963.

Protesters in the Great Hall of the hotel during the Democratic National Convention in August, 1968. While riots were occurring outside, the hotel served as a safe haven and makeshift hospital for the wounded.

*MP's guard the entrance to the Conrad Hilton during the
1968 Democratic National Convention.*

because the keys were nowhere to be found. The hotel had not been locked since 1927 when it was built as The Stevens Hotel. The full time locksmith on staff changed all the locks and keys."

As Smith further related, this did not completely solve the problem, even after it was determined that only those with keys would be allowed back inside the hotel. Senator McCarthy and his staff simply reproduced their keys and gave them out to his people and protesters in the park. As Smith said,

with some understatement, "Many more people entered the hotel than had a confirmed room." Ever the gracious host, "in true Hilton hospitality, employees brought chairs for them to sit in and offered them complimentary sandwiches." No one was arrested or convicted except for the McCarthy staff. Nick Costanzo, then a bellboy, remembered that police fed and cared for a baby while its parents protested outside. Costanzo recalled "a general sense of calm in the hotel, business as usual."

Former General Manager Gary Seibert recalls a story from a salesman who frequently stayed at the Conrad Hilton on business. In those days, there was a floor manager on every floor, usually a woman, who would always check your key. "Back then you would always have airline stewardesses in the hotel," the salesman related, "and it was my quest to get to a particular one of them. But how the heck could I do that with the female floor managers? Well one day I did, and that stewardess has been my wife ever since."

Behind-the-scenes: waiters prepare dessert in the Conrad's huge kitchen.

Part of the reason that the "Battle of Michigan Avenue" did not come through the doors of the Conrad Hilton was that the Normandie Lounge had been transformed into a makeshift M*A*S*H unit for the many injured protesters, police, and members of the press. Indeed, sympathizers hurled globs of ketchup at their colleagues in the park from the floors above in an attempt to get more of the "wounded" into the hotel. Sheets were taken from the rooms to use as bandages.

Following the tumultuous events of 1968, the Conrad Hilton returned to doing what it does best— welcoming guests in a comfortable and gracious manner. The hotel celebrated its 50th birthday in 1977 when, for a brief time, the popular ice skating shows were brought back to the Boulevard Room.

RECONSTRUCTION ON A GRAND SCALE

The great advances in information technology in the 1970s and 80s brought about significant changes in the way business was conducted, which in turn had a tremendous impact on the hospitality industry.

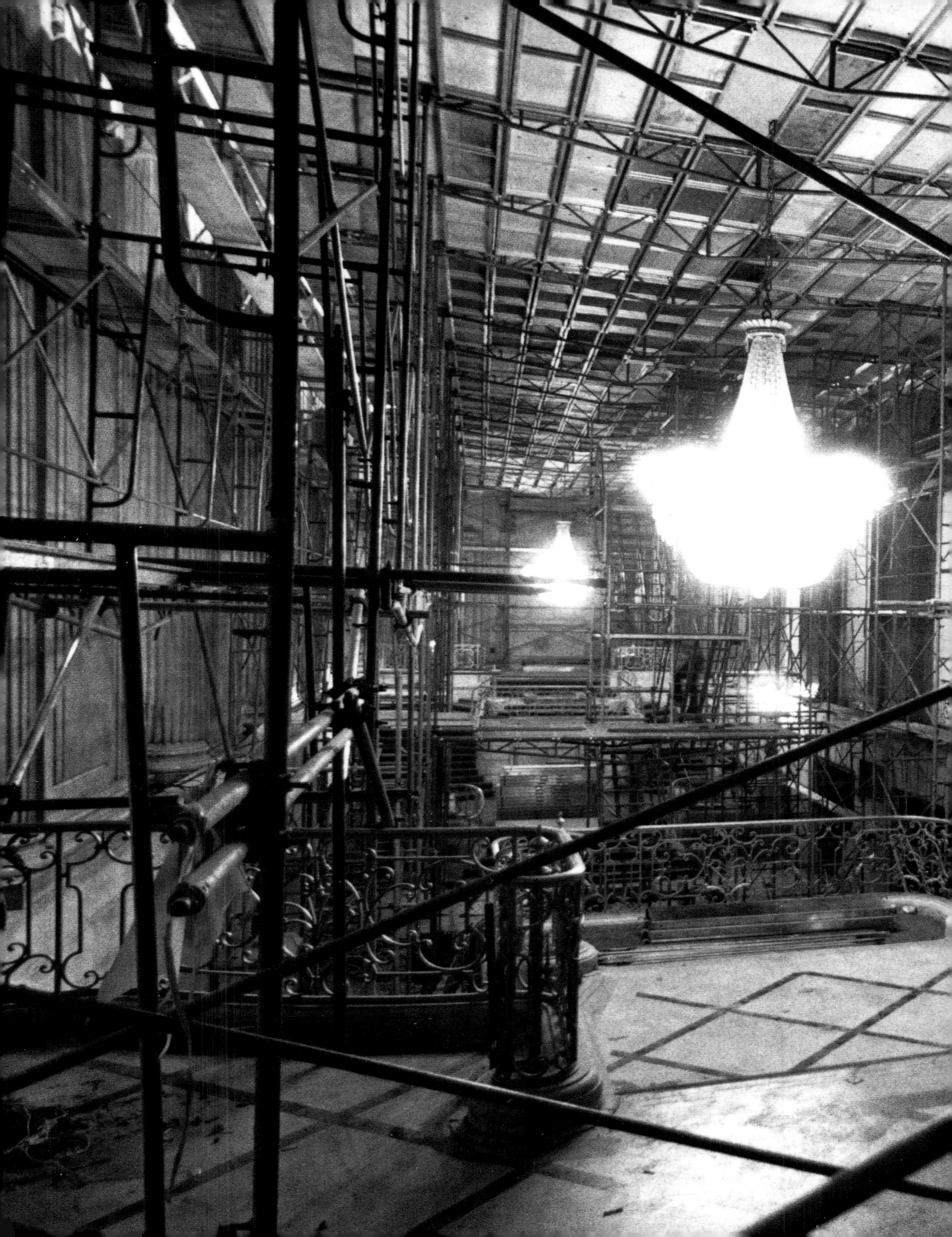

IT ALMOST DIDN'T HAPPEN

As with the uncertain fate of The Stevens following the withdrawal of the Army in 1943, the future of the Conrad Hilton was very much up in the air in 1978. "Has time passed the Conrad Hilton by?" questioned the Chicago Sun-Times on April 30 of that year. The Chicago Tribune may have unintentionally responded several weeks later when it described the Conrad Hilton's lobby as "gloomy" and "a little disappointing." An initiative laden with tax breaks nearly refocused the Hilton chain's attention to the North Loop of Chicago, where it would build a new hotel, allowing the Conrad to be converted into condominiums or offices. But the North Loop tax break that Hilton desired was ultimately denied, opening the door for the most expensive hotel renovation in history.

Worldwide, hotels had to adapt to the new demands of business and leisure travelers alike as faxes, electronic mail, and Internet access came to replace secretaries, typewriters, and "snail mail." To better serve the needs of the modern business traveler, the hotel room of yesterday thus had to be transformed into something of a hybrid guest room and office, with perhaps a small living area provided as well. The business traveler was spending more time in his or her hotel room working, entertaining, and of course sleeping. Even the whole concept of breakfast had changed, as many hotels started offering "grab and go" juice, coffee, and muffin bars in addition to traditional restaurant or room service fare.

The unique needs of a new type of guest—the traveling businesswoman—also had to be addressed. An inter-office memo from the Hilton's Suzanne M. Carney in 1982 anticipated many of the amenities first-class hotels were to add to appeal to this rapidly growing segment of the population:

Each room should include: hairdryers attached to the wall, magnifying mirror attached to the wall, skirt hangers, laundry line over the bath tub, plastic shower caps, extra fluffy towels, padded hangers, small sewing kit.
Each bathroom should have a small basket with shampoo, conditioner, hand lotion, Woolite, potpourri by Claire Burke, some type of shower gel and bubble bath.

These rooms should automatically have a complimentary turn down service each night with a Godiva chocolate on the pillow. If it's not too costly, a sweetheart rose on the visitor's nightstand should be placed on her pillow alongside the chocolate.

A traveling businesswoman does not want to stand out from her male counterpart. Therefore, you don't want to end up with a dorm type of situation where you have pink and peach rooms. Also, if she is interviewing or taking a deposition in her room (as many business people do), you'd want more of a neutral or professional look.

For economical and practical purposes, the rooms should be neutral enough in their décor that if the situation arose, they could be sold to men.

Consequently, the Conrad Hilton underwent what was called "the most comprehensive renewal project in hotel history." The renovation, which took place in 1984, not only cost an astronomical $185 million, but also shut the hotel down for over a year. No mere facelift, the hotel was literally rebuilt from the inside out. The 2,700 original guest rooms were gutted and transformed into 1,543 larger and more elegant rooms, 600 of which became "double-double" rooms with two marble and polished brass fixtured bathrooms. In the public areas old-world craftsmen painstakingly restored the 24-karat gold leaf, crystal, and marble appointments, and also the original oil paintings. Five new restaurants were created, one of which, Kitty O'Shea's, was a reconstructed Irish pub. A 510-car capacity parking

The Italian painter/restorer Lido Lippi spent seven months on scaffolding at the ceiling, cleaning Frescoes and repainting areas that had been severely damaged over the years. The fruit of his labors can be seen in the marvelously restored ceiling detail shown below.

garage was also added, as well as an athletic club with a large lap pool, a fitness room with the latest exercise equipment, a running track, whirlpool, and sauna. Parts of the first and third floors were made into an art museum to house the hotel's impressive $1.6 million collection of sculpture, oils, tapestries, watercolors and charcoal sketches. Assembled under the guidance of Alisa Witlin of Hirsch/Bedner and Associates and Audrey Brown of the 18th Street Gallery, the acquisitions brought the entire hotel collection to 2,300 pieces.

Detail of ceiling.

Renovation of the front desk.

General Manager Bill Smith conducts a site tour in the Normandie Lounge for the Chicago Lyric Opera Committee during the 1984-85 renovations.

The hotel was still somewhat functional during the renovation. Here General Manager Bill Smith and Executive Chef Wieland Ludwig conduct a taste test in the Grand Ballroom with members of the Lyric Opera Committee.

The task was daunting. Not only did lenders have to be convinced that restoration was better than simply knocking the structure down and building a new one in its place, but the blueprints for many of the changes and renovations over the years had not been saved. (The original plans from 1927 did exist, however.) For example, architect Jeff Orlove's preliminary plans for the renovation did not anticipate discovering not one but three ceilings concealed in the area where the two-story atrium was to be built. The removal of the ceilings further revealed railroad tracks in the substructure; evidently this was the area of the old Boulevard Room, and the tracks had been used to pull a stage over the ice rink. The ten- to twenty-foot rail sections had to be removed by torch. The cables that extended from the fifth to the thirtieth floor, once thought to be up to code, had to be completely replaced.

A more sensitive problem arising from the closing of the hotel for renovation was what to do with the existing staff. According to former Manager Eric Long, it was a very emotional time, since many of the people who had

The Grand Ballroom glows again following the renovation.

been employed by the hotel for as many as thirty or forty years now had to find new jobs. The Hilton management of course assisted them, and several former employees returned to the hotel once it reopened. However, to fill the remaining positions, Long had to take space at the McCormick Place Convention Center to conduct interviews and sift through over 10,000 applications.

Still, all obstacles were overcome, and the renovated, restored, and renamed Chicago Hilton and Towers reopened on October 1, 1985. Eric Long recalls that it all went "remarkably well. The construction crew that rebuilt it did so with great pride." Long soon after departed for the Waldorf in New York.

Grand Opening of the Chicago Hilton & Towers in 1985 presided over by Cook County Board Chairman, Richard Dunne.

So radical was the hotel's overhaul that many didn't even recognize it from its previous incarnations as either the Stevens or Conrad Hilton. The folk group Peter, Paul, and Mary, who were at the hotel during the 1968 riots, didn't realize (until someone informed them) that they were in the former Conrad Hilton when they performed in the Grand Ballroom during Bill Clinton's 1992 presidential campaign.

The crowning achievement of the reconstruction was the creation of The Towers, a "Hotel within the Hotel." Designed and planned for the truly discriminating traveler, the Towers offer special guests three floors of luxury. Its amenities include a private entryway; its very own concierge; two phones in each room; turndown service; a library; and its own lounge overlooking Lake Michigan for breakfast and evening cocktails.

MEETINGS AND CONVENTIONS GOLD KEY AWARD

Meeting planners vote for the top hotels and resorts throughout the world and selected the Hilton Chicago as one of the best! The Hilton Chicago is among the elite membership of Gold Key winners. The winners are voted on by the readers of Meetings and Conventions and are based on strict criteria, which include proficiency of handling reservations, quality of the meeting rooms, range of recreational facilities, quality of guest service, overall staff attitude, quality of food and beverage service and availability of technical/support equipment.

The dining room of the Conrad Hilton Suite.

The living room of the Conrad Hilton Suite.

However, perhaps the most extravagant hotel suite ever conceived is the Conrad Suite (briefly known as The Crown Imperial Suite), created during the renovation from the former ballrooms on the 29th and 30th floors and designed by Frank Mingis. The suite's design, construction, and furnishings alone cost $1.6 million, and include a grand salon with fireplace, dining area for fourteen, classic library, private kitchen, three bedrooms with full baths, two powder rooms, and four elevators for private access. Its two floors are connected by a spiral staircase, and ormolu, a metal alloy resembling gold, is generously applied throughout the suite to pilasters, moldings, and other furnishings.

The 1,880 square-foot grand salon on the 30th floor serves as a reception area, dining room, and parlor. The fireplace opens into both the dining room and connecting library. Four large windows offer spectacular views of the city's skyline and lakeshore, and further illumination is provided by four original gold and crystal Strauss chandeliers valued at $10,000 apiece. Large floral oriental rugs accent the hand-set mahogany parquet floors, which are composed of inlaid wood of three compatible fruit stains. Furnishings include oversized Louis XVI reproduction upholstered sofas and chairs, Queen Anne black lacquered low coffee tables, Chapman crystal lamps, and hand-carved Matteo D'Palermo tables.

The dining room of the Conrad Hilton Suite.

A grand piano graces the corner of the salon, and an original 11 X 13 foot seventeenth century Flemish tapestry depicting a hunting scene, valued at $35,000, dominates the dining area.

Easily the most popular room in the suite is the Breccia Onicita Marble-lined master bathroom, featuring a sunken jacuzzi overlooking the lake, private shower, and toilet room. A standard suite amenity is a bottle of champagne chilled and waiting in silver next to the jacuzzi.

All of this can be had for a mere $5000 a night. Maid, butler, and limousine service included, of course.

"The new Chicago Hilton and Towers is one of the most beautiful and gracious hotels in the world," General Manager Smith proclaimed after the renovation. "We're extremely proud of this renewed property and our pride is reflected through the attitude of our staff. They've earned us a leadership role. They've repositioned this landmark as one of the most distinctive in the world … ."

A A A   D I A M O N D   A W A R D

Each year, AAA/CAA tourism editors evaluate more than 30,000 lodging establishments throughout the U.S., Canada, Mexico and the Caribbean. Properties that meet AAA/CAA's requirements and represent members' travel needs are assigned a quality rating from one to five diamonds. In the past the Hilton Chicago has been awarded the Four Diamond status, which means the establishment is upscale in all areas. Accommodations are progressively more refined and stylish. The fundamental hallmarks at this level include an extensive array of amenities combined with a high degree of hospitality, service, and attention to detail.

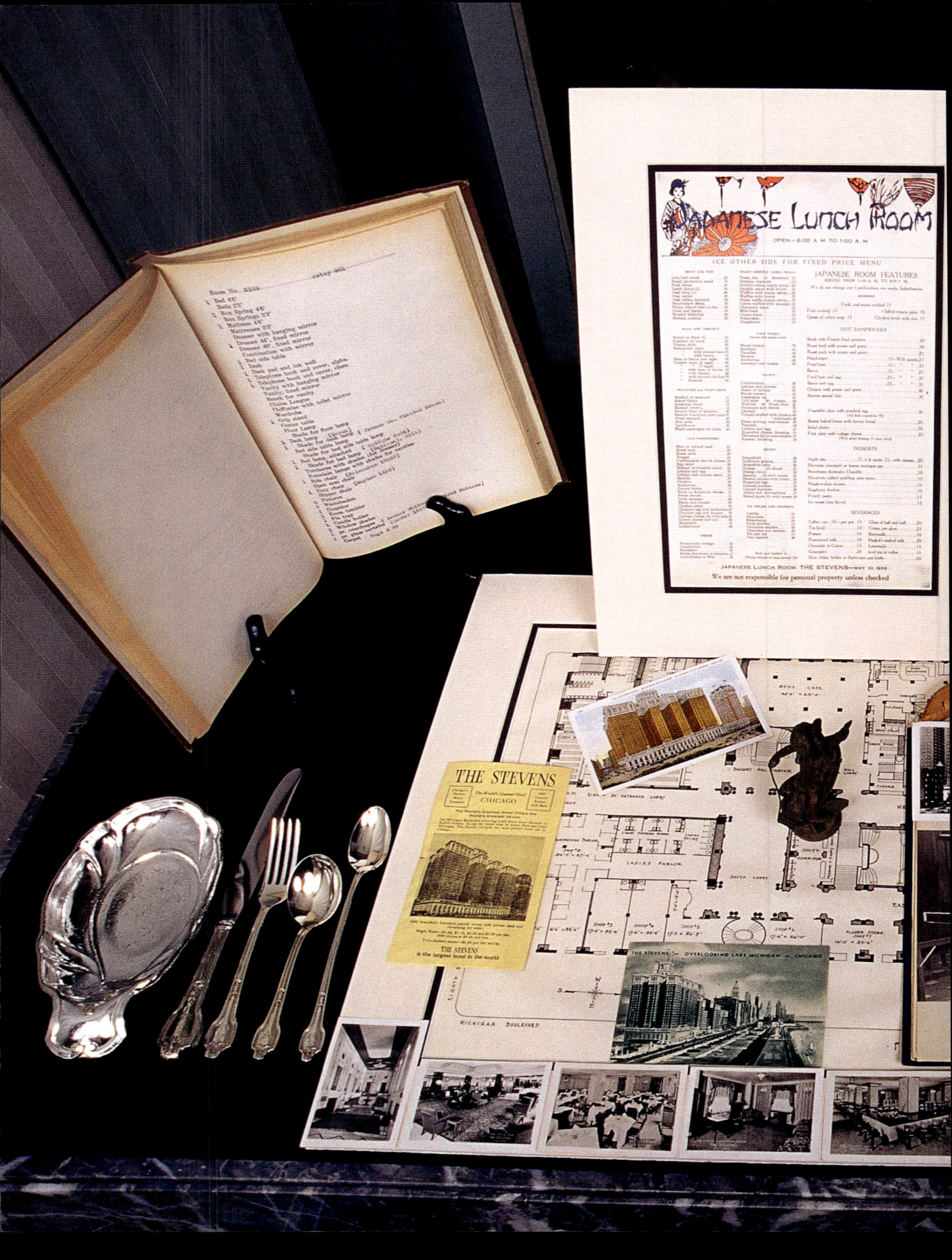

THE HILTON
BECOMES A STAR

When Kevin McAllister is reunited with his family at the end of the film "Home Alone 2," we are led to believe that the final scene takes place in a hotel suite in New York. In fact, the setting is the opulent Conrad Suite at the Hilton Chicago, the so-called "Midwest White House," where every president since Ronald Reagan has stayed. Indeed, since its renovation, the hotel has "starred" in no less than nine feature films.

The hospital heliport for the hit TV series "E.R." is actually the roof of the Hilton Chicago.

In 1993, the hotel gave a performance worthy of an Oscar nomination when it became the setting for the last twenty-five minutes of the blockbuster film "The Fugitive," starring Harrison Ford and Tommy Lee Jones. Shooting twelve hours a day for two straight weeks, the Warner Brothers crew filmed nearly every square foot of the hotel, from the roof promenade, to the Grand Ballroom, to the state-of-the-art laundry facility. Director Andy Davis and actors Ford, Jones, and Sela Ward became "regulars" after hours at Kitty O'Shea's, the hotel's Irish pub. (Ford even made an impromptu visit, as his alter ego Indiana Jones, to a gathering of Special Olympics children who had assembled in the International Ballroom for dinner one evening during filming.)

FILMED AT THE HILTON CHICAGO

MOVIES:
U.S. Marshalls
The Fugitive
My Best Friend's Wedding
Home Alone II
Primal Fear
The Package
Unconditional Love
Love and Action in Chicago
Road to Perdition

TELEVISION:
ER
Early Edition
Cupid

film concludes outside the entrance to the hotel as the camera pulls back to reveal the full majesty of the Hilton.

Former General Manager Gary Seibert recalls trying to keep the hotel operational during the occasionally chaotic filming. "We arranged with [Director] Andy Davis that if any guest was unhappy, he would have to make good on it, and making good on it was basically comping the room. One night they were running late filming a gun shot scene with the helicopter, and a guest who claimed he had been a veteran heard the shots and dove under his bed. The long and short of it was that the room was comped."

In the final, memorable chase scene of "The Fugitive," the action opens at the Michigan Avenue entrance to the Great Hall, then moves to the Grand Ballroom where Dr. Richard Kimble (Ford) confronts the man who has masterminded his wife's murder. Moving through the International Ballroom foyer directly to the Conrad suite, the two engage in a rough and tumble fistfight that carries them through the suite's library to the fire escape on the roof promenade. After falling through a movie-made skylight above an elevator shaft, the two resume their fisticuffs in the fifth floor laundry, where at last the Federal Marshall (Jones) catches up with both men after a suspenseful, nail-biting chase scene amongst laundry bags and bins. The

The choice of the Hilton Chicago as the setting for "The Fugitive" and other films is no mere serendipity; the hotel is actively marketed for this purpose because of its unique architecture and variety of filming locations, from its maze of sub-basements to the spectacular Conrad Suite. Moreover, the hotel is so large that filming of a major motion picture can take place without disrupting the normal business of the hotel. In fact, guests are often unaware that a famous movie or TV actor is in their midst. In January of 2000, for example, a convention of Chicago Cubs' fans sold out every room in the hotel for three days. At the same time, scenes from the television series "ER" were being shot on the hotel roof, which plays the part of the hospital roof and

CHICAGO *Hilton* and Towers

Photo by Stephen Vaughan

FOR IMMEDIATE RELEASE

Contact: Carol Gifford
Director of Public Relations
Chicago Hilton and Towers
312-431-6909

HARRISON FORD, "THE FUGITIVE," CAUGHT AT CHICAGO HILTON

Anna Collinge, Convention Service Manager at the Chicago Hilton and Towers catches "The Fugitive," better known as Harrison Ford, during the filming of the blockbuster movie, seen here in the Versailles-inspired Grand Ballroom. Warner Brothers filmed for two straight weeks at the hotel in more than 15 locations including the laundry facility, the roof and the Conrad Hilton Suite. In the end, the Chicago Hilton and Towers comes out with a starring role—the last 25 minutes of the movie.

720 South Michigan Avenue, Chicago, Illinois 60605   Telephone 312-922-4400
Reservations 1-800-HILTONS

Press release: Harrison Ford takes a break from shooting a scene from "The Fugitive" with Anna Collinge, Convention Service Manager. Warner Brothers filmed for two straight weeks at the hotel in more than fifteen locations, including the laundry facility, the roof, and the Conrad Hilton Suite. Indeed, the last twenty-five minutes of the film take place at the Hilton Chicago.

helipad in the popular NBC television drama. Few, if any, of the some 10,000 Cubs fans had any idea that Anthony Edwards (Dr. Mark Green) and Laura Innes (Dr. Kerry Weaver) were stomping around in the snow outside the Conrad Suite thirty floors above them. Or that Unconditional Love starring Dan Akroyd and Cathy Bates was being filmed in the sixth sub-basement of the hotel!

Befitting a movie set, the Hilton Chicago has hosted celebrities from all walks of life—world leaders, politicians, royalty, sports legends, and stars of the stage and screen. (A list of famous guests appears as an appendix to this book.) Former President Bill Clinton has stayed at the Hilton Chicago no less than six times while on visits to Chicago, and is evidently quite fond of the Conrad Suite's pool table. (He did stay at the Sheraton Chicago during the Democratic National Convention in 1996, but only because the Hilton Chicago was already designated as the media head-quarter hotel.)

If the many celebrities that have entered the doors of the Hilton have one thing in common, it's that they were probably served by veteran waiter Don Mavar, the hotel's "Banquet Captain to the Stars." A favorite among Secret Service agents because of his impeccable military record (1955-57), Mavar has been serving U.S. Presidents since he accidentally spilled salad on Harry Truman in 1951. A second generation waiter at the Hilton—his father Joseph emigrated to Chicago from Croatia and was hired as a banquet waiter at The Stevens in 1945—Mavar seems to have an anecdote or two about every president he has served. He recalls arriving at John F. Kennedy's suite with a bowl of oyster stew, only to find the president wearing nothing but blue polka dot boxer shorts. During a "dry" civic luncheon at the hotel, he snuck in some beer in a coffee cup at Kennedy's request. He caught some of Richard Nixon's off-color language following a fundraiser in the International Ballroom, an incident that instantly made Nixon the least favorite president he had served.

"The Secret Service and the White House have always enjoyed using the hotel for presidential visits or any other visits from heads of states," former General Manager (and current Palmer House G.M.) Gary Seibert recalls. "There are secured routes regardless of which way you're going, and over the years they have developed such a good rapport with the employees that they work with. I think it is a great compliment to the hotel and the staff."

left: Scene from Home Alone 2 *in the Conrad Suite*

right and below: Two shots from The Package

right: Tom Hanks takes a break from shooting Road to Perdition *with General Manager Tom Loughlin.*

Don Mavar, the hotel's "Banquet Waiter to the Stars", helps actress Helen Hayes with a birthday cake.

Mavar with Bob Hope.

Mavar with Luciano Pavaratti.

Don Mavar with presidential candidate Hubert Humphrey.

*Sam Cascio and former General
Manager Gary Seibert.*

*Former Hilton General Manager Gary Seibert (left) with Sam
Cascio, at age 95 the world's oldest working bellman. He worked
at the Hilton Chicago for 65 years, starting each day with a
"good cup of coffee and a shot of whiskey" prior to his two-hour
commute to the hotel. To his right is Cascio's protege Noel Walsh,
a forty-year veteran of the Chicago Hilton.*

THE ULTIMATE IN SERVICE

Noel Walsh, for over forty years a bell man at the Hilton, recalls the most unusual request from a guest he ever received:

"I remember getting a call. 'I'm in trouble,' said the caller, 'I just remembered I left my false teeth in the bathroom.' I got his room number, went to the room, found his teeth, and called a cab to deliver the man his teeth."

Gary Seibert with General Colin Powell after the Desert Storm campaign.

Mexican President Vincente Fox speaks at the Hilton Chicago in 2001.

Former General Manager Ken Smith welcomes British Prime Minster Tony Blair, while Herbert Nagel, former director of Hotel Security, keeps a watchful eye out.

Seibert with Republican Presidential nominee Bob Dole in 1996.

Kathy Cahill, Meetings and Convention Manager, greets the late John F. Kennedy, Jr. at the Physicians Against Landmines dinner.
JENNIFER GIRARD PHOTOGRAPHY

Ed Chen, Director of Catering, checks on regular guests Michael and Juanita Jordan at the Rotary International Gala held at the Hilton Chicago Hotel.

General Manager Thomas J. Loughlin greets Barbara Bush in 2001.

Aina Eglite, Assistant Director of Catering, welcomes the Premier of China, Zhu Rongji, in 1999.

Gary Seibert with former British Prime Minster Margaret Thatcher.

General Manager Gary Seibert with President Bill Clinton and First Lady Hillary Clinton.

Former President William Jefferson Clinton signs the VIP Guest Registry of the Hilton Chicago during a recent visit.

President Ronald Reagan signing legislation in the Grand Ballroom in 1984.

A DAY IN THE LIFE OF
THE HILTON CHICAGO

The Hilton Chicago's day starts with the rumble of trucks pulling up to the loading dock in the early morning, delivering the day's quota of fresh produce. At the same time, the in-house bakery prepares all of the sweet rolls and pastries that will be consumed at breakfast. In the floors above, room service attendants move quickly from door-to-door to collect all the "door hanger" breakfast menus while the night housekeeping staff finishes vacuuming and polishing in the public areas. As the first guests begin to rise, the manager of the Hilton Chicago Fitness Center opens the pool and exercise facilities.

above: The Great Hall.

The Grand Ballroom in dinner-dance mode.

A little later, hundreds of room attendants are given their instructions in pre-shift meetings. The front desk staff is informed about what groups will be checking into the hotel that day, and how they should be welcomed. Employees of the facilities department are setting up for the events that will occur that day as thousands of chairs are unloaded into the ballrooms for breakfast events. As many as ten separate breakfast meetings might be attended to by the hotel's banqueting department on a typical morning.

In the hotel's fourth floor executive offices, the senior management is already meeting to discuss which VIP's will be arriving at the hotel that day, and making sure that personal welcome cards are placed among their amenities. Room and catering sales executives arrive and work at their assigned tasks of keeping the hotel and its meeting rooms full. On the luxurious Executive Class levels of the hotel, guests are enjoying a continental breakfast overlooking Lake Michigan in the Towers Lounge. Far

The pool at the health and fitness center.

Kitty O'Sheas Irish Pub.

below in the convention halls, trade shows start to open, while at the same time—unseen and unheard—the hotel's massive laundry cleans, presses, and folds its own linens as well as those of the Palmer House.

In the afternoon the hotel lobby takes on the air of an elegant concourse as guests begin to arrive and check in. Special arrivals on any given day could include a foreign head of state, a famous actor, rock star, or even the President of the United States.

. . . .

One of our favorite pastimes is to unwind in the evening at the Hilton's Lakeside Green bar, and watch the cavalcade of human traffic as people from all walks of life enter the hotel from the porte cochère entrance on East Balbo Avenue. Here college students in blue jeans and sweatshirts headed for an Irish music "session" at Kitty O'Shea's mingle

A double/double guest room in the Hilton main house in 2000.

with civic leaders in tuxedos and evening gowns, dressed for some formal occasion in the Grand Ballroom. A romantic couple, attired in the clothing of the night, might arrive for a candlelight dinner at Buckingham's. Some Chicago Bears fans might join us at the bar to watch that night's game with the Packers. Sirens and a flurry of activity outside would herald the arrival of a dignitary or celebrity, but we won't see them—they arrive through a secret entrance known only to the

Hilton Chicago Executive Class guest room in 2000.

hotel staff. Meanwhile, in the floors below, a convention of booksellers is calling it a day, pouring into the Main Lobby in search of a libation and some friendly conversation.

Buckingham Fountain at Night with the Stevens Hotel to the Right

"My day is incredible," says current General Manager Tom Loughlin. "I start at 7:30 in the morning and tour the property and check agendas. Later on I might run a business meeting or greet a head of state. This business exposes you to an unlimited ceiling of opportunity. At the Hilton Chicago I consider myself the custodian of a rich tradition."

"One of the proudest moments I've had is when I entertained both my parents and my entire family here."

When viewed at night from Grant Park, the Hilton Chicago glows like a theater on opening night, a role it has played nearly every night for seventy-five years. Through its doors have passed American presidents, royalty, and celebrity; history has been made here. Indeed, so great is the legacy of the Hilton Chicago that it contains its own museum to itself, brimming with memorabilia from The Stevens era, to the Army occupation, up through the recent renovation.

A HOTEL TO THE STARS
AND ORDINARY PEOPLE ALIKE FOR
SEVENTY-FIVE YEARS, THE HILTON
CHICAGO IS ALSO A STAR, TAKING
A BRIGHT SPOT
IN THE CONSTELLATION
OF GRAND HOTELS
THAT HAVE MADE THEIR MARK
THROUGHOUT
THE WORLD.

U.S. PRESIDENTS & FIRST LADIES

Harry Truman

Dwight D. Eisenhower

John F. Kennedy

Lyndon Johnson

Richard Nixon

Gerald Ford

Jimmy Carter

Ronald Reagan

Nancy Reagan

George Bush

Barbara Bush

Bill Clinton

Hillary Rodham Clinton

OTHER DIGNITARIES

President of the Republic of Argentina, His Excellency Dr. Carlos Saul Menem

President of the Republic of Hungary, His Excellency Arpad Goncz

President of the Republic of Poland, His Excellency Lech Walesa

Prime Minister of Ireland, His Excellency Liam Cosgrave

President of Uruguay, Dr. Jorge Battle

President of Egypt, Anwar Sadat

President of South Korea, His Excellency Kim Dae-Jung

Premier of the People's Republic of China, His Excellency Zhu Rongji

President of Mexico, His Excellency Vincente Fox

First Lady of Mexico, Mrs. Martha Sahagun de Fox

Chief of Staff to President Reagan, John Sununu

Prime Minister of the United Kingdom, Margaret Thatcher

Prime Minster of the United Kingdom, Tony Blair

Prime Minister of Romania, Mugur Isarescu

Prime Minister of Israel, Simon Peres

Her Majesty Queen Noor of Jordan

Emperor Hirohito of Japan

Queen Elizabeth II of Great Britain

Prince Philip of Great Britain

His Majesty Carl XVI Gustaf, King of Sweden

Her Majesty Margrethe II and His Royal Highness,

Prince of Denmark

King Paul and Queen Frederica of Greece

Princess Aga Khan

Secretary of Defense Dick Cheney

Chairman of the Joint Chiefs of Staff Colin Powell

Vice President Nelson Rockefeller

Attorney General Janet Reno

Mayor Richard J. Daley

Mayor Richard M. Daley

Surgeon General C. Everett Koop

Minnesota Governor Jesse Ventura

Federal Reserve Board Chairman, Alan Greenspan

STARS OF THE STAGE AND SCREEN

Elizabeth Taylor

John Wayne

Yul Brenner

Pat O'Brien

Danny Thomas

Kenny Rogers

Grace Kelly

Jimmy Durante

Rock Hudson

Frank Sinatra

Gary Cooper

Richard Burton

Tony Bennett

Maria Callas

Betty Davis

Anthony Quinn

Elvis Presley

Walter Cronkite

Paul Anka

Helen Hayes

Jimmy Stewart

Liberace

Dean Martin

Richard Widmark

Zsa Zsa Gabor

Peter, Paul, and Mary

McCauley Culkin

Harrison Ford

Roger Ebert

Jack Lemmon

Marlee Matlin

Ray Charles

Willard Scott

Paula Poundstone

Jane Fonda

Michael Douglas

Glen Close

Michael Todd

Tony Martin

Luciano Pavorotti

Robert Wagner

Eddie Murphy

Gene Hackman

John Hurt

Joanne Cassidy

Tommy Lee Jones

Wesley Snipes

Stephanie Powers

Betty White

Bob Hope

Mike Wallace

Wolfman Jack

Victoria Principal

Liza Minelli

Dinah Shore

Smokey Robinson

Anita Baker

DeLa Soul

Keith Sweat

Malcolm Jamal Warner

Gregory Peck

George Benson

Rob Lowe

Billy Dee Williams

Daman Wayans

Milton Berle

Andy Williams

Rita Moreno

Shirley Jones

B.B. King

Koko Taylor

Johnny Cash

Bob Mackie

Douglas Fairbanks, Jr.

Luther Vandross

Marie Osmond

Sammy Davis, Jr.

Jane Seymour

Hugh O'Brien

Mel Torme

Harvey Korman

The Smothers Brothers

Jay Leno

Tony Danza

Debra Harry

Cher

Dianne Carroll

Rod Stewart

George Lucas

Patti LaBelle

Twyla Tharpe

Lou Gossett, Jr.

Estelle Getty

Richard Frank

Mary Tyler Moore

Sinbad

Dawn Lewis

Melissa Manchester

Joe Montegna

John Kander

Edward James Almos

Fred Ebb

Martin Landau

Elizabeth Perkins

Dixie Carter

Hal Holbrook

James Earl Jones

John Travolta

Morgan Freeman

Shelly Long

George Wendt

Michael Clarke Duncan

Joseph Bologna

Renee Taylor

Elliott Gould

Sally Kirkland

Rebecca Bush

Jere Burns

Karen Austin

Sidney Sheldon

Larry Manetti

Tom Selleck

Bill Cosby

Tom Hanks

U2

Rick Braun

Gregory Hines

Regis Philbin

Sigourney Weaver

The Beatles

Janet Leigh

Lauren Bacall

SPORTS LEGENDS AND OTHER HEROES

Amelia Earhart

Babe Ruth

Charles Lindbergh

Magic Johnson and the L.A. Lakers

Walter Payton

Michael Jordan

Merlin Olsen

Mike Ditka and the Chicago Bears

Chris Evert

Tracey Austin

Reggie Jackson

Ernie Banks

Joe DiMaggio

BUSINESS AND SPIRITUAL LEADERS

Ted Turner

Norman Vincent Peel

Lee Iacocca

Donald Trump

and many more too numerous to mention

Lauren Bacall.

Grace Kelly.

Bette Davis.

John Wayne.

President Eisenhower arrives at the Conrad Hilton in the 1950s.

Bing Crosby, Dolores Del Rio, and Bob Hope.

Babe Ruth.

Joe DiMaggio.

Elvis Presley.

The Fab Four at the Hilton Chicago.

"15,000,000," *The Economist* (Chicago), March 3, 1922.

"Brief History of Chicago's 1968 Democratic National Convention," in ALLPOLITICS 1996 [online database].

"Hotel Stevens Corner Laid," *The Hotel Bulletin*, April, 1926.

"U.S. Purchases the Stevens Hotel for 6 Millions," *Chicago Tribune*, December 13, 1942.

Bohn, Henry J. "The Fullfilling of a Prediction," *The Hotel World*, 7 May 1927.

Cahan, Richard. *Chicago: Rising from the Prairie*. Chicago: Heritage Media Corporation, 2000.

Dougles, Egbert and Cryster, Charles A. "The Mighty Power Plant," *The Hotel World*, 7 May 1927.

Gibson, B.K. "The Stevens Architecturally," *The Hotel World*, 7 May 1927.

Gilbert, Paul T. "A Personally Conducted Tour Through the Stevens." (no date).

Hilton Chicago. "Capsule Biographical Sketch: William L. Smith, General Manager, Chicago Hilton and Towers," undated press release.

Hilton Chicago. "Chicago Hilton and Towers Showcases 70 Years of Hosting History," undated press release.

Hilton Chicago. "Chicago Hilton and Towers' Conrad Hilton Suite Epitomizes Wealth," undated press release.

Hilton Chicago. "Chicago Hilton's Kitty O'Shea's Recreates Real Irish Pub Experience," undated press release.

Hilton Chicago. "Facts About the New Chicago Hilton and Towers," undated press release.

Hilton Chicago. "The Chicago Hilton Goes Hollywood," press release dated August 13, 1993.

Hilton Chicago. "The Whole World to Watch the Chicago Hilton during the Democratic National Convention," undated press release.

Hilton Chicago. "A Grand Tradition." Undated brochure.

Hilton, Conrad. *Be My Guest*. New York: Simon and Schuster, 1994.

Hoekstra, Dave. "Give this Captain a Gold Star," *Chicago Sun-Times*, October 25, 2001.

Interview with Associate Supreme Court Justice John Paul Stevens, dated May 17, 2002.

Interview with Eric Long, former Hilton Chicago General Manager, dated January 23, 2002

Interview with Gary Seibert, former Hilton Chicago General Manager, dated January 18, 2002.

Interview with Tom Loughlin, current Hilton Chicago General Manager, dated June 14, 2002.

Interview with Jack Lee, Hilton Chicago electrician, dated January 18, 2002.

Kart, Larry. "The Boulevard Room Gets Set to Take its Ice Out of Mothballs," *Chicago Tribune*, May 1, 1977.

Ludgin, Earle. "Creating the Perfect Hotel," *The Hotel World*, May 7, 1927.

Ludgin, Earle. "The Kitchens of the Stevens," *The Hotel World*, May 7, 1927.

Ratny, Ruth L. "Hotel to the Stars: Chicago Hilton and Towers a Unique Location for Filmmakers," *Screen*, August 31, 2001 [?].

Schuler, Loring. "A Very Grand Hotel," *The Saturday Evening Post*, June 17, 1944.

Stopping at The Stevens, December 24, 1931.

Stopping at The Stevens, May 14, 1927

Stopping at The Stevens, May 9, 1927.

Taylor, Eugene S. "Chicago and the Lake Front," *The Hotel World*, 7 May 1927.

"Where to Go and What to do When in Chicago," March 27, 1971

Robert V. Allegrini is Director of Public Relations for the Hilton Chicago, a position he has held since 1998. Allegrini is responsible for coordinating the hotel's media relations, community relations, and VIP guest relations. In this capacity he has hosted guests from around the world, including President Bill Clinton, British Prime Minister Tony Blair, Mexican President Vincente Fox, as well as entertainers John Travolta, Tom Hanks, Tom Cruise, and Lauren Bacall.

Prior to joining Hilton, Allegrini served seven years with Swissotel in Chicago, New York, and Seoul, Korea. Long active in the Italian American community on both the local and national levels, he was knighted in 1991 for his services to Chicago's Italian community by H.R.H. Prince Victor Emmanuel of Savoy.

Robert Allegrini received a bachelor's degree in Journalism from Norther Illinois University and attended graduate school for internation relations at the University of Florence in Italy.

Geraldine Hempel Davis's previous books include *The Today Show: An Anecdotal History, The Moving Experience,* and *Curves on the Highways: A Self Help Guide for Female Automobile Travelers.* She began a twenty-five year-long career in advertising, public relations, and television as the youngest producer assistant on the Ed Sullivan Show. Among other accomplishments, Davis has been a merchandising and marketing consultant for the Neiman Marcus Christmas catalog, and contributing correspondent to the Today Show.

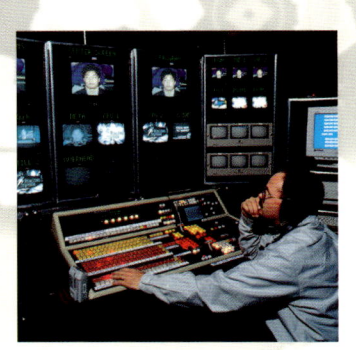

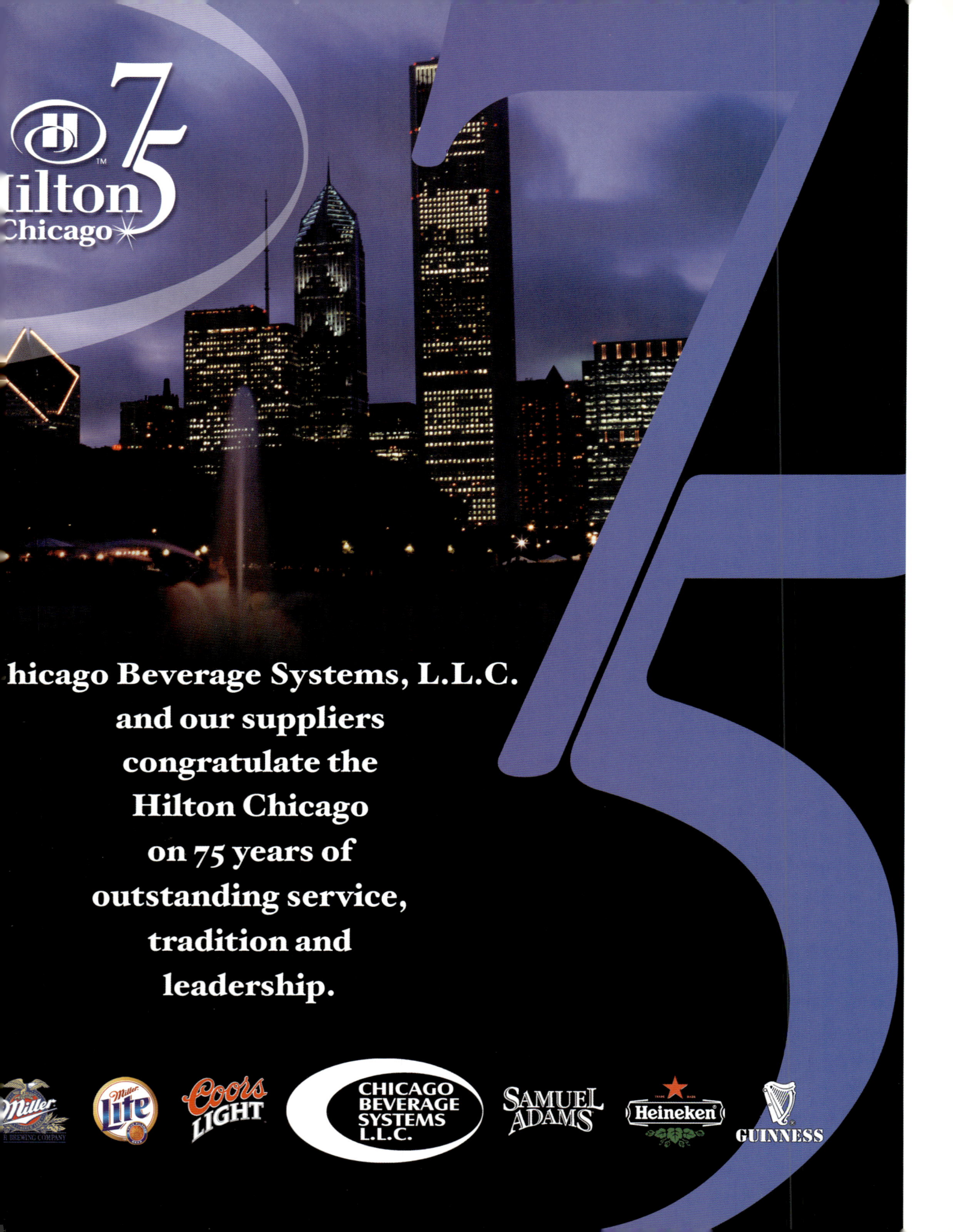

Danziger Kosher Catering

All of us at
Danziger Kosher Catering
would like to wish
congratulations to our
partners,
The Hilton Chicago on
their 75th Anniversary

"The Ultimate in Kosher Catering"
3910 W. Devon Avenue • Lincolnwood, Illinois 60712 • Tel 847-982-1818 • Fax 847-982-1178

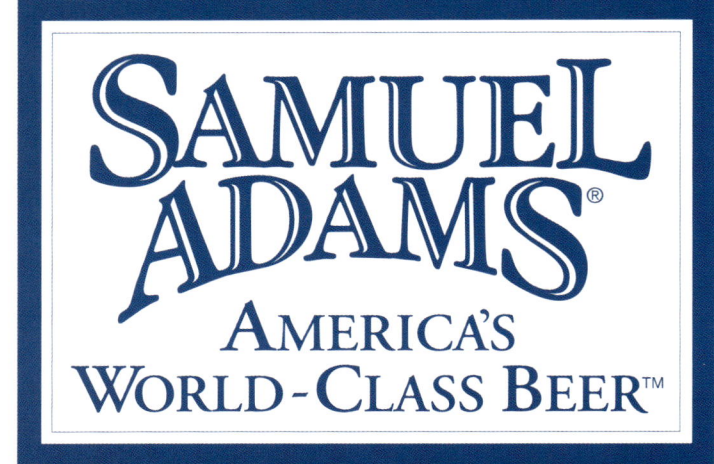

SAMUEL ADAMS®

AMERICA'S
WORLD-CLASS BEER™

Salutes

The Chicago Hilton Towers

on

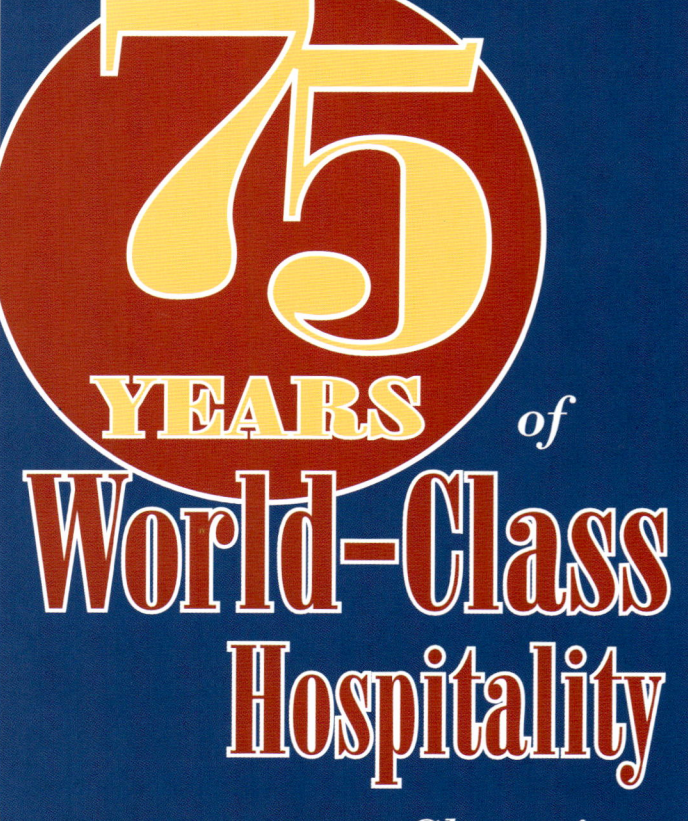

75

YEARS *of*

World-Class

Hospitality

Cheers!